MENTAL HEALTH FOR MEN

NEVER LOSING CONTROL

Stay Within Your Boundaries

Raul Reese

Table of Contents

Chapter 1: Mental Health Workbook 6

Chapter 2: The Importance Of Mental Health 10

Chapter 3: Stop Ignoring Your Health 14

Chapter 4: 7 Tips To Protect Your Mental Health 17

Chapter 5: 5 Habits of A Healthy Lifestyle 22

Chapter 6: 8 Habits That Can Kill You 27

Chapter 7: Affirmations For Men 33

Chapter 8: Types Of Eating Dissorders 43

Chapter 9: The Danger of Dwelling On Things 50

Chapter 10: How To Deal With Stress Head On? 53

Chapter 11: Ten Ways To Become Mentally Stronger 59

Chapter 12: Stop Worrying and Go To Sleep 64

Chapter 13: Stop Worrying and Get Well 67

Chapter 14: 5 Inspiration Stories For Men 70

Chapter 15: 8 Habits That Help You Live Longer 75

Chapter 16: 20 Positive Affirmations For Men 81

Chapter 17: Avoid The Dreaded Burnout 85

Chapter 18: Improving Your Sleeping Habits 88

Chapter 19: Meditate to Rewire Your Brain For Happiness 92

Chapter 20: Putting Exercise First 95

Chapter 21: 7 Habits Of Healthy People 98

Chapter 22: Why Seeking Habits Can Motivate You Better? 102

Chapter 23: Why Considering Theraphy Can Be An Option? 105

Chapter 24: The Healing Power of Nature 108

Chapter 25: The Downside of Work-Life Balance 112

Chapter 26: 6 Signs Your Mental Health is Getting Worse 115

Chapter 27: 7 Signs You Are Emotionally and Mentally Exhausted .. 102

Chapter 28: 8 Ways Of Stress Relief 125

Chapter 29: How To Deal With Stress 130

Chapter 30: 8 Bad Habits That Make You Age Faster 135

Chapter 1:

Mental Health Workbook

Mental Health

Mental health is simply the sanity of the mind. We need to have sane minds to be capable of living normal lives. Mental health is as equally important as physical health, maybe even more important. The mind is capable of many things even when the body is ailing but the reverse is not true.

Governments worldwide are emphasizing the need for their citizenry to observe their mental health. Nobody is safe from the pandemic that is bad mental health.

Relationships break daily and so do marriages and brotherhood bonds because of mental health issues. Not many people are ready for this talk that is why they keep jumping from one friendship to another. They hope things will be rosy in their next friendship only for the same script to play out again.

The good news is that it is not all gloomy. Something can be done about it.

Here is a mental health workbook:

1. Be Honest with Yourself

Honesty is very expensive. You can be dishonest with other people but never with yourself (this does not justify dishonesty with other people). Deep down in your spirit, you know the brutal truth about yourself. You just cannot bring yourself to accept reality.

Do your best to be honest about what is going on with your life. You are best suited for that because you know yourself all too well than anybody else does. Confront the evil thoughts in your mind and decide to change to become a new person.

If you are dishonest with yourself and you let the mental torment continue, it will grow bigger each day and become something entirely different. At this later stage, it will be unmanageable.

2. Accept Your Weakness and Work To Improve It

Once you have conquered the honesty stage, do not live in denial. Accept your weakness but do not accept to continue living with it. Well, quite a few people manage to skip the denial stage part. They continue to refuse that they are mentally tortured by unspoken evil thoughts.

Indeed, we can never want to turn out to be bad people. It is never who you are but circumstances are molding you to become someone you are not. Accept that you are a candidate for mental health issues and start addressing them in a personal capacity while you still can.

3. Be Your Own Manager

Understandably, some people (especially a majority of men) are not good at opening up to other people about their problems. In this case, assume the role of managing yourself.

It is a difficult position to assume because you are most likely going to be lenient with yourself. As the manager of self, you have to make important decisions like cutting off friendships with toxic friends because they are bad influences. Most of the time this is something you know but you cannot bring yourself to do it.

Be a ruthless and decisive manager. Your mental health will thank you for this later on.

4. Seek An External Unbiased Opinion About Yourself

You can be your own manager but hardly an unbiased judge. After the three above steps, now is the time to seek someone else's opinion. At this stage, you must have already seen some changes in your mental health. Certain aspects must have started to change. Your initial view about things has been renewed. However, you need to bring someone else to establish credibility to your progress.

Rope them in your mental health journey. It must be somebody who knew you before and after this moment because they can clearly spot the difference.

5. Start Over or Celebrate Your Win

This is based on the results of the previous stage. What was the verdict of the external 'referee'?

If they concluded that there is a remarkable change, then bingo! You won this one. You successfully recovered from slipping into mental health issues.

If there is still no change, then you have two options: either start the process again or seek professional help.

This mental health workbook is efficient if you pay attention to it. Follow through every step carefully for the best results.

Chapter 2:

The Importance Of Mental Health

Health Is Wealth

Good health is man's biggest treasure. It is priceless and invaluable. The irony is that many wealthy people are victims of long-term diseases like high blood pressure and diabetes. If money could buy good health, they could buy it because they can afford it.

Everyone can fall sick yet no amount of resources can buy good health. This is a call to everyone to protect their health. Good health involves physical, emotional, and mental health. Each of them is equally important. We should always protect them.

Mind Over Body

The human mind is in charge of decision-making and motivation towards goals. When likened to a game of chess, mental health is like the king who is protected by the queen, knights, bishops, and pons. When the king is captured, it is game over.

When your mental health is affected, all aspects of your life come to a halt. You can neither do business well nor work properly. Your interpersonal relationships are broken because you can assault those around you.

The Supremacy of The Mind

Good mental health is important to everyone. It informs the competence of a person for a particular task. People go to schools and training institutions to learn skills. The mind facilitates learning.

Good mental health optimizes the working of the mind. Apart from being a measure of intelligence, the mind is a source of innovations. Simple to complex innovations is all products of the mind.

Mental health is important to those whose physical and emotional health is affected. It provides the willpower to stay strong despite their illness.

Care Of Mental Health

The journey of taking care of our mental health begins with recognizing how important it is. It informs the decisions we make and the direction of our lives afterward. Some of the ways of mental health care are:

1. Self-Love

It is appreciating yourself more than other people do. Rejection never bothers you because you understand your worth. In self-love, bad opinions of other people about you do not affect your psychology.

Self-love promotes mental health. You accept your weaknesses and embrace your strengths when you learn to love yourself. Self-love should not be mistaken for selfishness. It is prioritizing your mental health before other things.

2. Emotional Intelligence

It is emotional maturity to see through blackmail and true emotions. Sometimes we allow the emotions of other people to affect our psychology. This is inappropriate because some emotions could blackmail us to assume the guilt of things, we had no control over.

Emotional intelligence saves us from depression and anxiety. Although emotional maturity comes with time, it is possible to develop it from a younger age. Practice separating your mind from emotions. Allow only important matters to reign in your mind.

3. Know Your Limits

Understand your limits and position in the lives of people. You will not outdo yourself trying to impress people who do not care. You will infringe on the personal space of people when you interact too much with them.

Set boundaries as you interact with other people and focus on yourself. Do not allow other people's problems to affect your mental health. You can only help when necessary but do not shoulder their burden.

4. Lower Your Expectations

It is fine to have dreams and targets, but it is not okay to have high expectations. They can cost you peace of mind when not met. Play your part and allow nature to take its course. Expectations are normal especially as you plan for something.

In planning, you expect results at a certain stage. However, limit your expectations and let the good results shock you. You can change your plans when you do not meet your targets.

In conclusion, the importance of mental health cannot be underscored. These four health care tips will create good mental health. Follow them through for the best results.

Chapter 3:

Stop Ignoring Your Health

Do you have a busy life? Do you follow a hard and continuous regime of tasks every day for a significant amount of time? Have you ever felt that you cannot enjoy even the happiest moments of your life even if you want to? Let me highlight one reason you might recognize it straight away.

You are not enjoying your days while still being in all your senses because you don't have your mind and body in the right place.

All these years you have lived your life as a race. You have taken part in every event in and around your life just because you never wanted to miss anything. But in this process, you never lived your life to its full potential. You never lived a single moment with just the emotional intention of being then and there and not trying to live it like just another day or event.

People often get so busy with making their careers that they don't realize what is more important in life? It is their mental and physical health!

You will not get anywhere far in your life if you keep ignoring the signs of sickness your body keeps giving you. Your body is a machine with a conditional warranty. The day you violate the conditions of this warranty, life will become challenging, and you won't even be interested in the basic tasks at hand.

You might have heard the famous saying that "Health is Wealth". Let it sink in for a while and analyze your own life. You don't need to be a top-tier athlete to have a good body. You need a good body for your organs to work properly. You need an active lifestyle to be more productive and be more present and engaged in the things that are going around you.

The dilemma of our lives is that we don't care about what we have right now, but we care a lot about what we want. Not realizing that what we want might be cursed but what we have is the soul of good living. And that my friends are the blessing of health that most of us take for granted.

Most people have a tendency and devotion to work specifically on their health and fitness on a priority basis. They have a better standard of life. These people have a clearer mind to feel and capture the best moments in life with what their senses can offer best to them.

If you don't stop ignoring your health, you won't ever get out of this constant struggle. The struggle to find the reasons for you being detached from everything despite being involved every time.

Being careful and observant of your health doesn't make you selfish. This makes you a much more caring person because not only your life but the life of others around you is also affected by your sickness. Not only your resources are used for your treatments but the attention and emotions of your loved ones are also being spent, just in hope of your wellness.

Chapter 4:

7 Tips To Protect Your Mental Health

We're living in times where everyone is waking up to the daily barrage of upsetting news. From the global pandemic to the enormous omicron wave to the war in Ukraine, there has been a lot going on. It is normal to feel stressed, fearful, anxious, frustrated, lonely, and even angry amid a pandemic, safety, and economic crisis. However, if these issues are not addressed, they can progress into more serious mental health issues that can impact your emotional, psychological, and physical well-being.

Mental health is responsible for your line of thoughts, feelings, and behaviour. Such that, interconnectedness of your thoughts, emotions, or feelings and how you behave says more on how stable your mental health is. In simpler terms, mental health influences how you deal with stress, interacts with others, and make decisions at all stages of your life. It is therefore vital that you learn how to keep your mental state healthy.

Here are 7 tips to protect your mental health.

1. Know That You Are Not Alone

Even up-to date, the topic surrounding mental health is still not openly embraced. People rarely express their feelings and instead try to suppress their negative thoughts and emotions, leading to harmful coping mechanisms. Everyone has had a difficult time in recent years, so know that you are not alone. Seek professional help if necessary and remember that anxiety and stress are normal and pose no dangers when managed.

2. Wellness Is Being All-Rounded

The principle of well-being is much more than just being physically healthy. It is an integration of your mind and the body with your circumstances. Embracing changes and uncertainties, nurturing your mind and body, building resilience, learning, and growing, and doing something meaningful. Although there is no single way of maximizing your mental well-being, self-care practices such as sleep, taking nutritious food, exercise, mindfulness, or meditation, or having a "me time" will help protect your mental and physical health.

3. Hold Genuine Conversations

Maintaining a healthy and happy mind requires removing yourself from unhealthy or toxic relationships altogether. It also implies keeping close a positive support system instead of withdrawing completely from other people. Isolation is unhealthy but connecting with people profoundly and honestly is capable of improving your overall well-being. Make a conscious effort to keep in contact with the people who bring you joy.

4. Stop Self-Medicating

If you are someone who goes for hooks such as alcohol, drugs, caffeine, or sweets to feel numb or increase your energy, you are harming your mental health. Don't succumb to the temptation of the "happy hour" as it will only worsen the situation. Excessive consumption of alcohol, caffeine, or drugs has been linked to frequent anxiety attacks. It's time to try your "new go-to" to boost your endorphins and dopamine levels.

5. Step Back and Take Deep Breathes

Several factors influence how healthy you're psychologically and physically. It is very easy to get caught up in making ends meet that you forget to embark on the simple things that protect your well-being. Maintain a meaningful struggle by limiting your focus to one or two things that matter most. Delegate some if need be and direct your energy on doing something good for your well-being.

6. Practice Gratitude

It's imperative to take a moment and appreciate the fact there was a time when you had a great experience. Appreciating the little things allows you to see life in a new light. For example, if you are stressed, focus your attention on the tiny things that once brought you joy. Practicing gratitude allows you to remember all the positive experiences.

7. Be King to Your Sweet Self

Research conducted by psychologist Kristin Neff has demonstrated the importance of treating yourself compassionately in coping with emotional issues and distress. To alleviate these feelings, acknowledge your struggles with kindness rather than beating yourself up or judging yourself. Avoid worsening the situation than it is already.

Conclusion

Whatever is going on with you, keep in mind that your mental health is crucial. Whatever you're dealing with, protecting your mental well-being is critical if you want to be productive and happy. Create some time for yourself and do everything it takes to overcome stress.

Chapter 5:

Five Habits of A Healthy Lifestyle

A healthy lifestyle is everybody's dream. The young and old, rich and poor, weak and strong, and male and female all want a happily ever after and many years full of life. The price to pay to achieve this dream is what distinguishes all these classes of people. What are you ready to forego as the opportunity cost to have a healthy lifestyle?

Here are five habits for a healthy lifestyle.

1. Eating Healthy Food

Your health is heavily dependent on your diet. You have heard that what goes inside a man does not defile him, but what goes out of him does. In this case, the opposite is true. What a man takes as food or beverage affects him directly. It can alter the body's metabolism and introduce toxins in the body, hence endangering his life.

Most people do not take care of what they feed on. They eat anything edible that is readily available without any consideration. All other factors like the nutritive value of the food and its hygiene are secondary to most modern people who have thrown caution to the wind. Towns and cities are full of fast-food joints and attract masses from all over. It is the most lucrative business these days. Are these fast foods healthy?

As much as the hygiene could be up to standards (due to the measures put in place by authorities), the composition of these foods (mostly chips and broiler chicken) is wanting. The cooking oil used is full of cholesterol that is a major cause of cardiac diseases. To lead a healthy lifestyle, eating healthy food should be a priority.

2. Regular Exercising

The human body requires regular exercise to be fit. Running, walking, swimming, or going to the gym are a few of the many ways that people can exercise. It is a call to get out of your comfort zone to ward off some lifestyle diseases. It is often misconstrued that exercising is a reserve for sportsmen and women. This fallacy has taken root in the minds of many people.

Unlearn the myths about exercises that have made most people shun them. The benefits of exercising are uncountable. It improves pressure and blood circulation in the body. Exercises also burn excess calories in tissues that would otherwise clog blood vessels and pose a health hazard.

Research has shown that most people who exercise are healthy and fall sick less often. This is everyone's dream but the few who choose to pay the price enjoy it. Choose to be healthy by doing away with frequent motor vehicle transport and instead walk. A simple walk is an exercise already. When you fail to exercise early enough, you will be a frequent patient at the hospital. Prevention is always better than cure.

In the words of world marathon champion, Eliud Kipchoge, a running nation is a healthy nation.

3. Regular Medical Checkup

When was the last time you went for a medical checkup even when you were not sick? If the answer is negative or a long time ago, then a healthy lifestyle is still unreachable. A medical examination will reveal any disease in its early stages.

In most third-world countries, healthcare systems are not fully developed. Its citizens only go to the hospital when a disease has progressed and is in its late stages. At such a time, there is a higher probability of the patient succumbing to it. Doctors advise people to seek medical attention at the slightest symptom to treat and manage long-term illnesses. Regular medical checkups help one become more productive at work.

Is a healthy lifestyle attainable? Yes, it is when one takes the necessary measures to fight diseases. Regular medical checkups can be financially draining. Seek an insurance policy that can underwrite your health risks, and this will make medical expenses affordable.

4.   Staying Positive

A bad attitude is like a flat tire. If you do not change it, you will never go anywhere. There is a hidden power in having a positive attitude towards life. It all starts in the mind. When you conceive the right attitude towards life, you have won half the battle.

A healthy lifestyle starts with the mind. If you believe it, you can achieve it. So limitless is the human mind that it strongly influences the direction of a person's life. As much as there are challenges in life, do not allow them to conquer your mind or take over your spirit. Once they do, you will be constantly waging a losing battle. Is that what we want?

Associate with positive like-minded people and you will be miles away from depression and low self-esteem. We all desire that healthy lifestyle.

5.   Have A Confidant and A Best Friend

Who is a best friend? He/she is someone you can trust to share your joy and sadness, and your high and low moments. You should be careful in your selection of a confidant because it may have strong ramifications if the friendship is not genuine.

A confidant is someone you can confide in comfortably without fear of him/her leaking your secrets. He/she will help you overcome some difficult situations in life. We all need a shoulder to lean on in our darkest times and a voice to comfort us that it is darkest before dawn. This helps fortify our mental health. We grow better and stronger in this healthy lifestyle.

These are the five habits for a healthy lifestyle. When we live by them, success becomes our portion.

Chapter 6:

8 Habits That Can Kill You

Toxic habits in our lives which when left unchecked can lead us to an early grave. We may not be aware of it, but it is most definitely eating away at us slowly; like a frog gradually boiling to his death. These invisible yet harmful habits will start appearing in your life if you don't start taking note of it.

Here are 8 habits that can kill you if you're not careful:

1. Being a Workaholic

Man shall eat from the sweat of his brows. Our income pays our bills and puts food on the table. This infers that work is good for it is the backbone on which our survival is pegged upon. It is however not a license to bite more than you can chew. Drowning yourself at work is dangerous for your health.

There is a breaking point for every person. Workaholism is a habit that depressed people do to drown their misery. With only so much that you can handle, you will lose touch with the world if you work without a break. Workaholics are not hard workers who work to make ends meet. They are obsessed with work so that they can forget their problems.

If you are a workaholic who uses business to distract you from your problems, you run the risk of sinking to depression. Take note if stress disorders or suicidal thoughts start to appear. It may be time to seek help to deal with your problems head on instead of making them in busyness.

2.   Isolating Yourself From Others

Withdrawal is a red flag any day, anytime. The moment you begin finding comfort in solitude, not wanting to associate with anyone, a problem is in the offing. However, there are times when you will need time alone to meditate and seek peace within yourself.

It is during withdrawal that suicidal thoughts are entertained and sometimes executed. When one isolates themselves from the rest of the world, he becomes blind and deaf to the reality on the ground. You seemingly live in a separate world often mistaken as one of tranquility and peace.

To fight isolation, always find a reason to be around people you share common interests with. It could be sports, writing, acting, or watching. This will help keep off loneliness.

3. Drug and Substance Abuse

Drug abuse is a pitfall that many youths have fallen into. It will lead you to an early grave if you do not stop early enough. Apart from the long-term side effects on the health of addicts, drug abuse rips addicts off morality. Most of them become truants, finding themselves on the wrong side of the law and society.

Among the many reasons drug addicts give for drug abuse is that drugs give solace from the harsh world, some kind of temporary blissful haven which the soul longs for. It is unjustifiable to enter into such a health-damaging dungeon to contract respiratory diseases, liver disease, kidney damage, and cardiovascular diseases.

Be careful if you seek drugs as a way to escape from your troubles. If you look closely, most of these people do not end up in a good place after abusing these substances. Seek a healthier alternative instead to let off steam instead.

4. Judging Yourself By The Standards of Others

As Albert Einstein rightly put it; if we judge a fish by its ability to climb a tree, it will live its whole life believing it is stupid. It is erroneous to use other people's measurement of success to judge your own. This is not to say that you should not be appreciating the achievements of others, but as you do so, give yourself time and space for growth.

The pressure that comes with conforming to your peers' standards can push you down a dark path. Society can be so unforgiving for the faint-hearted. Once you are inside the dark hole of hopelessness, the air of gloom hangs over your head and it can lead you to an early grave. Everyone will forsake you when you fail even after trying to be like them.

5. Being In The Wrong Company

Bad company ruins good morals. This truth is as old as civilization. It is not rocket science on how powerful the power of influence from friends is. When in the wrong company, you will be tagged into all sorts of activities they do. Isn't that a direct ticket to hades?

When you lose the power to say No and defend your integrity, morals, and everything that you believe in, then all hell will break loose on you. You would have handed your hypocrite friends the license to ruin your life. Not only will the wrong company ruin your life but also assassinate your character. Keep safe by fleeing from the wrong company when you can before it is too late.

6. Lying

It looks simple but what many people do not consider is the effect of character assassination caused by a simple lie. Lying makes you unreliable. One client or employer will tell another one and before you know it no one wants anything to do with you.

It may not physically kill you, but it will have the power to close all possible open doors of opportunities. Why not be genuine in your dealings and win the trust of your employers and clients? You should jealously protect your reputation because any assault at it is a direct attack on your integrity.

7. Lack of Physical Exercise

A healthy body is a healthy mind. To increase your longevity, you need to have a healthy lifestyle. It is not always about the posh vehicle you are driving or the classy estate you live in. How physically fit you are plays a big role in determining your productivity.

You need to walk out there in the sun, go for a morning run, lift weights, do yoga and kegel exercises, or go swimming. Your body needs to be maintained by exercise and not dieting alone. It seems ignoble to be a field person, but its benefits are immense.

8. Poor Nutritional Habits

The risks of poor nutrition are uncountable. Overeating and obesity come from these habits. Few people pay attention to what they eat, ignorant of the consequences that follow.

Malnutrition and obesity are opposites but stemming from one source – poor nutrition. The eminent danger can no longer be ignored.

According to statistics from the World Health Organization, worldwide obesity has nearly tripled since 1975. In 2016 alone, more than 1.9 billion adults were overweight. The world health body acknowledges that the developmental, economic, social, and medical impacts of the global burden of malnutrition are serious and lasting, for individuals and their families, communities, and countries.

This has come as a shocker to us, but it would not have been so if people paid attention to their nutrition habits.

All these 8 habits that can kill you are avoidable if caution is taken. The ball is in your court. Consider carefully whether you want to make a conscious decision to take responsibility and eliminate these damaging habits. You have the power to change if you believe in yourself.

Chapter 7:

Affirmations For Men

It is true that things have a course of action, and that everything has a cycle. This is true for every one of us. We all grow, and we all prevail. Sometimes we all get distracted and reach a point where don't want to take it anymore and just want to be left alone.

We have lived long enough to come to terms with the way things are and the rituals of the world. We should be able to appreciate things as they stand right now. We should be able to look for the good in everything in and around us.

It does get hard more than often, and we just want things to get a bit easier, but they never really do. The fog of self-doubt and constant failure make it hard to look for the bright edges, but here is when the positive affirmations play a vital role.

Affirmations are the things you say and do to make yourself feel more alive and remind yourself that you have more in your life than you think you don't.

We all have these small quotes or commands that we give to ourselves for the sake of growing in every hard time. We tell ourselves that we have to stand form in these rough times and one day we will grow tall and above all these swamps of uncertainty.

We men have a lot on our plate, and we go through a ton of grind in our everyday life. It is easy to lose sight of our habits and our passions when we are presented with a barrage of hardships. But never can we afford to get washed away will all the beating in the world. Because we are strong beings, and we need to stay strong for not only us but also the people that depend on us.

How to Create Your Own Positive Affirmations?

So how do create these feelings of self-motivation, these quotations of deep dedication, these positive affirmations?

What do you need for an affirmation to have an impact?

I have created four clear criteria for each affirmation to meet.

l the first one, obviously your affirmation should be optimistic.
l Secondly, whatever you create, it should be in the present.
l Your affirmations should be specific to a particular problem or a particular goal.
l Lastly but most importantly, all your affirmations should be related to yourself.

The best affirmations that you can create are the ones that are derived from a negative habit or ritual. But how change things around?

How can you take something negative and change it into a positive statement to make you grow?

How can you make these positive affirmations? Or if you have some already, how can you make them work for them?

Let's start it the other way around. Let's say you think that you are not good at your job. You think that you are not being as successful as others. You think that you are not worthy of success. You need to let go off of these thoughts. The longer you hold on to them, the more you will drown in the sorrow and the less capable you will be to get the position you always dreamed of.

Stop thinking: "I am not performing well. I cannot be the employ of the month. I am not getting the raise this year". Instead, start thinking: "I am a competitive employee. I can get the job done before time. I will get all the bonuses this year."

The minute you start to think positive, you will feel a surge of completeness and wholesomeness.

Let me help you craft some positive affirmations for yourself.

Let's start with a general and most basic one,

"From this day onwards, I am going to bid farewell to every bad memory and every regret. I have nothing to be ashamed of as I am only a human."

You are trapped inside a body that is smart but has its restrictions. We all make mistakes, and this is what makes us mortal.

You cannot live a life of fear and regret. You cannot possibly be charged with punishment for every little mistake that you make consciously or unconsciously.

"I am Strong and resilient, and I can make my own choices. No one can control me by their opinions about me or others."

"I am confident about my body and its true limits. I can push my limits to where ever I want them to be."

"I am valued by my loved ones, and they can help me be a better version of myself."

"My feelings and my emotions are as important as anyone else's. I have a right to be heard and I will always raise my voice for the right cause."

"I am worthy of Mental and Monetary stability and peace."

Can I Create My Own Meditation Mantra?

"I deserve more for my efforts, and I deserve appraisal and success for my hard work."

"I am an emotional being and no one can judge my manliness on this. I have all rights to share my feelings and tears if I am feeling down."

"My strength is my ideas and I have some great ones. I can express my concerns with full responsibility as I have my experiences and knowledge to back them."

"No one can reach my inner core and change it. Neither will I let anyone do that."

"I deserve to be happy, and I deserve the abundance in life that I have longed for."

"I can achieve any goal in life, and no one can tear me down till I remain strong and keep my intentions neat."

"What I have lost is what was meant to go, but what I want is meant to be mine."

"Some challenges I can take head-on. The ones I shouldn't engage in, I know when to walk away from those."

"I can make new friends, I just need to believe in people."

"I can walk away from toxic friends, I just need to gather some courage and speak out my heart."

"People will get impressed once they get to know me better. I can prove to be a great friend for anyone who wants my company."

"Good things will happen for me if I stay loyal to my cause, and I will not let anyone stand in my way."

"I am a magnet to new opportunities, and I am ready to do everything new and scary that looks me in the eye today."

"I can be resilient, and I am resilient. I always learn from my mistakes, and I keep moving forward."

"I define my purpose and that purpose is carved within. No one sketches my purpose and my path for me."

"I say what I deem right and what I say is right. No fluff and no bluff."

"Bad things will always happen, but I will always be able to make the best out of every bad situation."

"I am a proud being with a lot to look back on and a lot to look up to."

"I don't need anyone to stand up for me or to justify my decisions. My actions and their consequences will answer for themselves."

"I am not perfect, but I can try to be the best I can be."

"My worth is not what others think of me. My worth is the people that depend on me and the ones that look up to me."

"I am more than capable of achieving greatness as long as I stick to my basic goals and the rest will be history."

"I don't have space for humility in my life. I am proud and content with whatever I have right now."

Remember the Fundamentals

"I don't need anyone else to measure my greatness and my abilities."

"No one is more resourceful than me and I am the greatest asset anyone can have."

"I have to create my own calm and get rid of all my untroubled past."

"I am a good father, a good brother, a good partner, and a good friend."

"I am the bravest person I know. No one can declare me a coward and a quitter."

"My spirits are on their highest every day I wake up."

"I am thankful for everything I have done today, and I have am more grateful for what I shall do better tomorrow."

"No goal is small, and I am determined to fulfill all my legitimate desires no matter what cost I have to pay for them."

"My life has all the meaning in it already, I just have to look around all the corners."

"I should start every day with a positive feeling and end every day with a better one."

"I cannot change anyone or their perceptions about me, but I can change my response towards them."

"I don't need anyone to boost my confidence. I am the biggest cause and source of my inspirations."

"Happiness is not a choice; it is my obligation towards myself and others."

"My efforts and my intentions will eventually pay off, no matter how hard the world tries to turn me down."

"No one can judge me on my looks or my age. My history has worth no matter how short or long it is."

"I am a learner, and I will always be a work in progress. I don't expect me to be perfect."

"I have great respect for my body and everything in it. The things I can do with it are the blessing for which I can never be grateful enough."

"I can compete with any coworker at any level, but no one can tell me when to."

"Whoever needs my help shall find me standing and fighting beside them at every rough corner."

"I have left all my baggage behind, and I won't have any to drag me down ever again."

"My workout sessions will keep my mind and my body engaged for the greater good of a long and healthy life."

"I fulfill all my duties and I deserve all the love and respect in return."

"My smile is enough to keep my sorrows away and it will someday be a source of light for someone else in need of happiness."

"I need to learn to say 'No' without needing to explain myself. The best weight I can lose is the weight of other people's opinion of me."

Words are just words and if you don't put them to good use. Life is a rough ride. A little more for some and a little smooth for the others. But the jitters are all the same for everyone.

You can have a good functioning life even if you don't have something to look out for in life. But the purpose of life is not fulfilled if you learn the process.

Life was never meant to be lived like a script written by a robot. Life has a lot of things that are dynamic and a little more complicated than sleeping, getting up, eating, working on a timetable, eating again, and finally back to sleep.

We need to create more things in life where we have a lot more to live for and new ways to cherish life. We need to find meaning in every aspect of life. We need to find productive relationships and productive hobbies. We need to defend our rights and our actions. We need to open up about our emotions and our struggles. We need appreciation and we all need the warmth of humanly touch. But what we can't do is to keep a distance from everyone that loves us or everyone that wants to pin us down.

Keep reminding yourself of these affirmations every day and you won't have a day in your life when you don't feel a spark that keeps you going in life.

We have a duty towards ourselves to make the best out of everything in life till the time we finally close our eyes and say our goodbyes to this world!

Chapter 8:

Types of Eating Disorders

Eating disorders are behavioral conditions characterized by a severe change in eating behaviors mainly because of distressing thoughts and emotions. Eating disorders negatively impact your health and psychology. Every aspect of your life is affected by it and it can cause severe health problems leading to death if left untreated.

The Scope of Eating Disorders

As with every other mental illness, anyone can be a potential victim of eating disorders. However, there are target groups that are mostly affected by individual types of eating disorders e.g., adolescents, young adults, women, and old people.

Some of the known causes of eating disorders are:

1. **Genetics** – people who have close relatives suffering from an eating disorder are more prone to developing one.

2. **Personality Traits** – some traits are toxic and likely to put you at the risk of developing an eating disorder. People with

habits like perfectionism want to have a 'perfect' eating plan. They end up doing more harm to themselves than the good they intended.

3. **Cultural Influences** – In some cultures, it is taboo to gain weight. Members of that particular community will do anything including skipping meals.

4. **Exposure to Media** – Media influence to be thin and overemphasis on the outward appearance of a person plays a bigger role in the rise of the number of cases of eating disorders

Signs of Eating Disorders

You should be alert to identify the onset of an eating disorder and address it before it is too late. Many signs point to this. They include:

- Over exercising.

- Over emphasis on healthy eating.

- Skipping meals.

- Eating in secret.

- Feeling guilty or shameful about your eating habits.

- Extreme concern about your outward appearance (your size, weight, and shape).

Types of Eating Disorders

1. Anorexia Nervosa

It mostly develops at the onset of adolescence and affects more women than men. This is probably because these groups are the most conscious about their outward appearance and will go to extra lengths to fit in with the rest.

People with Anorexia nervosa usually think they are overweight even when they are not. They constantly check their weight and restrict themselves from taking certain foods. However, this is not the only criteria for judging that one has this type of eating disorder. Their thoughts are almost always preoccupied about food and what they can do to have that perfect body.

2. Bulimia Nervosa

Unlike those suffering from anorexia nervosa, those with bulimia nervosa tend to have episodes of binges. They eat a lot of food in a very short time until they become very full and cannot continue anymore.

Thereafter, they try to induce vomiting after they are already full because they feel guilty and ashamed of their behavior. Some even resort to using laxatives and diuretics.

3. Binge Eating Disorder

It is very close to bulimia nervosa. The major difference is that those suffering from this type of eating disorder do not try to 'undo' their over feeding by inducing vomiting or using laxatives and diuretics.

They eat a lot of food and do not even think of nutritional value. To them, it is quantity over quality. Although it increases their risk of medical complications, they have no control over their eating habits unless they seek treatment.

4. Pica

This disorder involves eating things that are not considered food and have no nutritional value. It presents itself in form of cravings for dirt, soil, ice, paper, cloth, hair, stones, and other non-food items.

People with this type of disorder are at an increased risk of poisoning, infections, or internal body injuries. For a condition to qualify as a pica eating disorder, eating non-food items should not be because of your religion, culture, or social acceptance by your peers.

5. Rumination Disorder

Rumination eating disorder is when a person regurgitates swallowed food, chews it again, and either swallows it for the second time or spits it out. This disorder can develop at any stage in life (infancy, childhood, or adulthood).

It can cause malnutrition when the food is finally spat out or when the affected person decides to eat less to stop this bad eating disorder. It is however treatable when addressed timely.

6. Avoidant/Restrictive Food Intake Disorder(ARFID)

This disorder is mainly characterized by a total lack of interest in eating. You begin not seeing the importance of eating and subsequently fail to meet your daily nutrition requirements.

Those with this disorder can be very choosy about what they want to eat. They discriminate food based on color, smell, or just develop a bad attitude towards it. Unlike other eating disorders, those with ARFID do not avoid food because of the fear of gaining weight.

Treatment of Eating Disorders

Like other psychological illnesses, eating disorders are treatable with the correct approach. Understand that those who suffer from them are victims and when given an opportunity they would want to be healthy again.

Known methods of treatment include:

- Seeking an audience with those who suffer from eating disorders.

- Acknowledge their feelings instead of victimizing them.

- Be respectful and avoid shaming them.

It could be you or someone you know who suffers from an eating disorder. The earlier you seek professional help the better. Knowledge about eating disorders will help reduce the stigma involved.

Chapter 9:

The Danger Of Dwelling On Things.

Do you ever go through a phase where you constantly replay old events in your head or worry and fret about what you could have done differently in a particular situation? Or do you obsessively dwell on past events and keep on repeating a loop of overthinking about your problems? Well, you might think that you're being productive by trying to solve your issues, but in reality, it does more harm than good to you.

There is a specific word for the above situation, and it is "Rumination." Ruminating is the process of dwelling on past events that can't be changed. People who have an anxiety-prone personality are more likely to experience this than others. Some examples include replaying conversations, repeating the past negative experiences in your mind, dwelling on injuries or injustices, and always asking seemingly unanswerable questions of "why me?" In all instances of rumination, the point is that the person gets stuck on a single subject, experience, or emotion.

Yale University conducted research that showed women are more likely to ruminate than men, leading to women having a higher risk of depression. Additionally, the study also focused on the fact that rumination prevents people from acknowledging and dealing with their emotions; they try to understand the situation instead of focusing on the feelings that the situation has caused. The impact of rumination is dangerous and is often underestimated. It is also given the name of "the silent mental health problem." It can play a significant role in anything from obsessive-compulsive disorder (OCD) to eating disorders. According to the World Health Organization (WHO), mental health affects one person in every four during their lifetime and is the leading cause of disability globally. In 2010 alone, they were estimated to have cost $2.5 trillion globally by the World Economic Forum.

Dwelling your past and never escaping the loop will affect you negatively that will eventually eat you alive. Some things might help you to overcome this problem. The first is to self-evaluate and dedicate time to whatever it is that's bothering you. Write all your thoughts down on a piece of paper or the notes app on your phone and set aside some time to think about it. Imagine the worst-case scenario that could happen from your dwelling, and then find a way that how you will deal with it. It will eventually leave you calmer and less anxious because a solution would already be in your hands.

Identify your anxiety triggers and the patterns that eventually lead you to rumination. Once you have identified it, focus on what you would do the next time to avoid making those mistakes again. Talking to a friend would be a good solution too. Write about the things that make you happy and the things you are grateful for. Revisit the list every day and focus on the positives.

It may be easier said than done, but accept that everyone makes mistakes, and it's in the past. You have learned from the situations, and now you have to let go and move on. It may not be easy at first but practice it every day. The more you practice, the easier this process will become, and you will eventually find your peace.

Chapter 10:

How To Deal with Stress Head On? 7 Things You Can Start Today

Drop your shoulders, release your tongue from your palate. Unclench your teeth and let your brows relax. You see, this is how stressed you are all the time, you forget completely about how it is affecting your body.

In this roaring river of the 21st century, we are all feeling the tide rising and falling 24/7. It will be a white lie if any of you claim to never feel stressed. We are all under varying degrees of stress all the time.

So, what is stress exactly? Stress is not merely a stimulus or a physical response of our bodies but a process by which we appraise and cope with environmental threats and challenges. When expressed in short bursts or taken as a challenge, stressors may have positive effects. However, if stress is threatening or prolonged, it can be harmful for us.

So how then do we handle it?

It seems like quite a drag for most of us and pretty annoying a lot of the time, but here are several ways we can deal with it and come out of it stronger than before.

7 Tips to Deal with Stress and Anxiety

Number 1: Go to Bed Early and Wake up Early

Have you heard the quote "Early to Bed, early to rise, makes a man healthy, wealthy and wise."? When was the last time you went to sleep early? I believe that going to bed early is something we all know we need to do but hardly ever do.

Starting your day off early has many wonderful biological effects. Mornings tend to be cool, silent, serene, and distraction-free. This calmness helps bring our stress levels down and prepares us for the day ahead. By practicing some deep breathing techniques in the morning, it will also aid in flow and circulation throughout our bodies, something that is good for the mind and soul.

Number 2: Start Practicing Yoga or meditation

Yoga and meditation, while they are two separate practices, they overlap in many key areas. Yoga poses are great for us to engage with our bodies, to stretch out our muscles, tight sections of our bodies, and to help us focus on our breath at all times. Each yoga pose targets a unique meridian of our bodies, many allowing us to release tensions that might otherwise have built up without realizing. You can try simple poses such as a child pose or shavasana, or downward dog, to get yourself started.

Meditation on the other hand focuses stilling the mind through focus on the breath as well. Letting our thoughts flow freely, we are able to acknowledge the stressors we face without judgement. Try out some guided mindfulness meditation practices to get your started.

Number 3: Having Proper Time Management

Many of us overlook the importance of proper time management. We often let our crazy schedules overwhelm us. By being unorganized with our time, we are also unorganized with our emotions. If we let our calendar be filled with chaos, there is no doubt that we will feel like chaos as well. Stress levels will be bound to rise. Have proper blocks of time dedicated to each task in your day. Trust me you will feel a whole lot more in control of everything.

Number 4: Make Time For Your Hobbies

We should all strive to live a happy and balanced life. If work is the only thing on our agenda, we will have no outlet to destress, relax, recharge, and be ready to face new challenges that might tax our physical and mental abilities.

Whatever your hobbies are: baking, tennis, crafting, surfboarding, or even shopping, as long as you plan them in your schedule and do them, you will definitely feel a whole lot better about everything. Let out all the steam, stress, anxieties, as you engage in your hobbies, or even just forget about them for a minute. Give yourself the space to breathe and just enjoy doing the fun things in life. Life isn't just all about work. Play is equally important too.

Number 5: Music Is Food For Your Soul

Music has many therapeutic qualities. If you feel your stress levels rising, consider popping your earbuds into your ears and playing your favorite songs on Spotify. If you are looking for calm, you may want to consider listening to some chill music as well.

The kind of your music you listen to will have a direct effect on your mood and the way you feel. So, choose your playlists wisely. Don't go heavy metal or goth, unless of course it helps calm you down.

Number 6: Start Cleaning Your Clutter

This may seem like I am quoting a movie where the stressed teenage girl decides to clean her room when she is feeling low. I'd say movies are made out of someone's real experience.

Cleaning your room or clutter can be one of the best therapies.

A messy space is a recipe for anxiety and stress. When we see clutter, we feel cluttered. Once you clear all the stuff you don't need, you will feel much lighter instantly.

Number 7: Allow nature to heal you

Nature is amusing and wonderful. Everything in nature is closer to our basic making than anything that we are dealing with today. So, try getting close to nature, it will make you feel relaxed and at the same time enable you to enrich your brain.

Watch the sun setting into the sky and wake up to look at the colors at dawn.
There is nothing more beautiful in this world that we get to experience every single day no matter where we are on this earth.

Take a stroll in your favourite park, go for a cycle, a jog, or even just a stroll with your pet. Allow nature to melt away your stress and bring your peace.

Final Thoughts

Stressors are a part of life. Something we cannot escape from. But if we put in place some healthy habits and practices, we can reduce and release those negativities from our bodies, cleansing us to take on more stress in the future.

Chapter 11:

Ten Ways To Become Mentally Stronger

Mental strength is a very great asset. Seek to grow it daily and you shall stand out from the crowd. There is one true test of knowing your mental strength. Seek to know the honest opinion of people whom you have interacted with. They can assess you better on how you responded to issues that required your attention. The good news is that there are tried, tested, and proven ways on how you can increase your mental strength.

Here are ten ways:

1. Having Healthy Debates

Debates form an important part of growing your mental strength and social skills. There are two sides to every debate. Persuading your opponents that your position of the matter being discussed is the right way and not theirs is an uphill task. You cannot shout them down to submission or physically pull them over to your side. Listen to good debaters' debates and watch how they ask very important questions. Your mental strength grows as you engage like-minded people in critical thinking. It takes one sharp mind to strengthen another because iron sharpens iron.

2. Taking Interest In Mathematics and Science

All subjects are equally important. Mathematics and science just engage the mind a little bit more than others. These subjects involve a lot of logic and accurate analysis which is why they are fit to strengthen your mind. Start reading scientific theories that explain the difficult phenomenon. This will make you question what you considered normal. You will become mentally stronger with every analysis you make.

3. Learn to Accept Defeat

A mentally strong person knows that defeat is an important part of learning. It means you have not got it right but learned another way of how not to do things. Defeat will not break you down when you accept it as part of life. You emerge stronger every time people expect you to succumb to it.

5. Believe in Philosophy or Religion

Philosophy and religion hold very important pillars for society. They seek to explain what is a mystery to date. The creation and evolution stories are examples of theories developed to explain the origin of man. When you follow either of them, you will ask hard questions about particular beliefs that most people hold to date. This is your path to freedom of your mind!

5. Play Mind Games

Do you know that all work without play makes Jack a dull boy? An important part of the play is mind games. They include reverse psychology intending to get other people to reveal their true intentions. Mind games help build a strong mind because you can penetrate the mind of another person through a simple conversation. You study their responses and attitude to life, and you can choose whether or not to keep them as friends.

6. Improving Your Concentration

How long and how deep you can concentrate on a single subject is very important. You should be capable of doing that for a longer period than the average person if you want to be mentally stronger. Do not give in to distractions when you are focusing on something. Think about its breadth and depth. Consider all the variables present and you will be able to make the right choice.

7. Understanding Over Cramming

Many people will choose to cram over understanding because it is the shorter route. Yes, it could be shorter but it reduces your mental strength. A mentally stronger person can explain a new concept in their words as they understood it. Students who understand their teachers instead of cramming what they are taught are mentally strong. Make an effort to understand new things even if it is in small parts. The mind can never be full. You can only be tired, but you can resume from where you paused it.

8. Keep the Company of Mentally Gifted People

Other people are mentally gifted. They understand new concepts the moment they are taught. Their analysis of everything is excellent and you can hardly find a fault with their thinking patterns. When you hang out with them, you will be able to study their thinking and approach. You can borrow a few skills from their prowess. Knowledge, like foolishness, is contagious. Beware of your company.

9. Embrace Challenges

Mental strength can increase or decrease. It is dependent on one major factor – challenges. Do not run away from challenges. Face them head-on. The same challenge will not come to you twice and it will leave you better than how it found you. This does not mean you should go looking for trouble. Only handle whatever comes your way. Have an open mind that the challenge you are facing is a lesson in preparation for your next step in life.

10. Meet New People

Making new friends is not entirely a bad idea. Strangers can turn out to be best friends and even family! Your mind should be exposed to how different people run their things and their different approaches towards life. New people offer new experiences. These will strengthen your mind and approach to diversity.

Conclusion

The mind is like a muscle. Do not be afraid of committing mistakes. They offer a correction point of getting it right the next time. Practicing these ten ways will leave you mentally stronger.

Chapter 12:

Stop Worrying and Go To Sleep

What are we meant to do when we have had a long day and we are finally on our bed but cannot sleep? We cannot let go of all the headaches we go through every day all day long. How can we reset the memories or only the guilt and remorse that we keep carrying each day?

We all want to give up everything for just a good night's sleep, but rarely do we get to enjoy one. We all want everything to be simple and easy for just a short while but, the reality is we are ready to let go!

I know that life is not a fairy tale, and we all have harsh realities that need to be dealt with. But why is that we can't let it get easy even when nothing is wrong in our life?

We are so used to taking pressure that sometimes we feel normal to be so sucked into these unnecessary and unhealthy things. Don't get me wrong, but the pressure is important. Pressure makes you feel like a human and makes us feel like we are the superior of all beings. But staying under the pressure by choice is something that you should never get accustomed to.

Why is it that you are always in need of searching for something that keeps you away from happiness? You have made this false scenario in your head that if everything is wrong and if you close your eyes for just one small moment, everything might turn upside down.

This behavior has spun this emotional roller coaster in us, that does not let us give up on anything even when we are at our lowest.

You have to understand a simple concept. You are an integral part of everyone's life around you. But you are no good to them if you cannot live a long, happy, and healthy life. A life in which you have not dedicated enough time to them, by sharing their feelings and your pain with them.

You need some time off not only for your well-being but indirectly, for them to have you in their lives.

You have to get rid of your past. Get rid of your pains for just a portion of your day or night in that case. Just so you don't seem like a life-less moving object, who talks only when you ask them something.

Be open, be transparent, be indulging, be engaging and be interesting so that you are worth caring for. You cannot expect sympathy and emotions if you are not willing or are not capable of giving something in return.

For that, you need to give your brain some time to shut down and reset. Your brain has an optimal limit to work on its peak, so does your body.

Your body and your brain work in sync to make you look like a proper human being. So don't get in your way to happiness and satisfaction.

So, drop all your anxieties and worries and go to sleep. If you have regrets about doing it, think of it as you are paying back to your body and your loved ones. Paying back for everything that they do to keep you safe and active.

Chapter 13:

Stop Worrying and Get Well

Humans have a gift that most take for granted; it's the brain!

You see, we have a bank of memories for which you don't need to spend anything and the limit is practically none. And we take advantage of that. We fill up our brains with things that don't necessarily need to be put in there.

We have a false sense of imagination of this world where we look at everyone as if they always want to harm us. We have created this false reality where everything seems like going against us. It's not healthy to live a life feeling like an outsider everywhere you go.

What you are doing is a reality that no one wants to be a part of. But you have included everyone in it without them having to do anything with everything going on in your life!

You are looking for something that you don't even have the slightest clue about. You are looking for the satisfaction of some sort. You are looking for a sense of security that everything is OK, and you don't need to worry about it. But you keep on worrying about it while trying to forget it.

Let me help you set a path to ease your anguish. You want a positive attitude towards life and people. You think you lack the optimistic approach towards life. This is a somewhat true assumption!

But let me assure you. You don't need to be positive first. You need 'Clarity'!

You want everything to be perfect, but you are not even sure what is it that you want to prioritize first. What is it that you want the most? What is it that you need to let go of first? What are the things that worry you the most?

You can't have this attitude that everything needs to be perfect. Everything can't go according to your taste. You want everything to go as planned, but your mind can't possibly comprehend everything that might happen to you in your life. Neither any failure nor any success.

So how can you be so naive? You don't need surety, you need a clear perspective of what is important and what you need to do about it. The rest isn't related. At least for now!

You need to prioritize your health first. Think about it! If you cannot let your brain squeeze out the unimportant harmful memories or scenarios of what could possibly happen.

You have to focus on what is now and what is important. You have to have a new vision of life, your past, your present, and your future.

Most people are not suffering at the hands of life. They are suffering within their memories and these false realities that they create themselves.

You have to learn to differentiate between what is reality and what is that you have been imagining for the longest part of your life. If you can't learn to make your mind differentiate between these things, your mind will become your greatest enemy and most certainly the hardest to get rid of!

Chapter 14:

5 Inspiration Stories For Men

These 5 motivational stories will encourage you to follow your dreams, treat others with kindness, and never give up on yourself.

1. Laziness Won't Get You Anywhere

"In ancient times, a king had his men place a boulder on a roadway. He then hid in the bushes and watched to see if anyone would move the boulder out of the way. Some of the king's wealthiest merchants and courtiers passed by and simply walked around it.

Many people blamed the King for not keeping the roads clear, but none of them did anything about getting the stone removed.

One day, a peasant came along carrying vegetables. Upon approaching the boulder, the peasant laid down his burden and tried to push the stone out of the way. After much pushing and straining, he finally managed.

After the peasant went back to pick up his vegetables, he noticed a purse lying in the road where the boulder had been. The purse contained many gold coins and note from the King explain that the gold was for the person who removed the boulder from the road."

2. Don't Say Something You Regret Out of Anger

"There once was a little boy who had a very bad temper. His father decided to hand him a bag of nails and said that every time the boy lost his temper, he had to hammer a nail into the fence.

On the first day, the boy hammered 37 nails into that fence.

The boy gradually began to control his temper over the next few weeks, and the number of nails he was hammering into the fence slowly decreased. He discovered it was easier to control his temper than to hammer those nails into the fence.

Finally, the day came when the boy didn't lose his temper at all. He told his father the news and the father suggested that the boy should now pull out a nail every day he kept his temper under control.

The days passed and the young boy was finally able to tell his father that all the nails were gone. The father took his son by the hand and led him to the fence.

'You have done well, my son, but look at the holes in the fence. The fence will never be the same. When you say things in anger, they leave a scar just like this one. You can put a knife in a man and draw it out. It won't matter how many times you say I'm sorry, the wound is still there.'"

3. Stop Wasting Your Time Complaining

"People visit a wise man complaining about the same problems over and over again. One day, he decided to tell them a joke and they all roared with laughter.

After a few minutes, he told them the same joke and only a few of them smiled.

Then he told the same joke for a third time, but no one laughed or smiled anymore.

The wise man smiled and said: 'You can't laugh at the same joke over and over. So why are you always crying about the same problem?'"

4. Damaged Souls Still Have Worth

"A shop owner placed a sign above his door that said: 'Puppies for Sale.' Signs like this always have a way of attracting young children, and to no surprise, a boy saw the sign and approached the owner; 'How much are you going to sell the puppies for?' he asked.

The store owner replied, 'Anywhere from $30 to $50.'

The little boy pulled out some change from his pocket. 'I have $2.37,' he said. 'Can I please look at them?'

The shop owner smiled and whistled. Out of the kennel came Lady, who ran down the aisle of his shop followed by five teeny, tiny balls of fur.

One puppy was lagging considerably behind. Immediately the little boy singled out the lagging, limping puppy and said, 'What's wrong with that little dog?'

The shop owner explained that the veterinarian had examined the little puppy and had discovered it didn't have a hip socket. It would always limp. It would always be lame.

The little boy became excited. 'That is the puppy that I want to buy.'

The shop owner said, 'No, you don't want to buy that little dog. If you really want him, I'll just give him to you.'

The little boy got quite upset. He looked straight into the store owner's eyes, pointing his finger, and said.

'I don't want you to give him to me. That little dog is worth every bit as much as all the other dogs and I'll pay full price. In fact, I'll give you $2.37 now, and 50 cents a month until I have him paid for.'

The shop owner countered, 'You really don't want to buy this little dog. He is never going to be able to run and jump and play with you like the other puppies.'

To his surprise, the little boy reached down and rolled up his pant leg to reveal a badly twisted, crippled left leg supported by a big metal brace. He looked up at the shop owner and softly replied, 'Well, I don't run so well myself, and the little puppy will need someone who understands!'"

5. Never Let One Failure from The Past Hold You Back in The Future

"As a man was passing the elephants, he suddenly stopped, confused by the fact that these huge creatures were being held by only a small rope tied to their front leg. No chains, no cages. It was obvious that the elephants could, at anytime, break away from their bonds but for some reason, they did not.

He saw a trainer nearby and asked why these animals just stood there and made no attempt to get away. 'Well,' trainer said, 'when they are very young and much smaller, we use the same size rope to tie them and, at that age, it's enough to hold them. As they grow up, they are conditioned to believe they cannot break away. They believe the rope can still hold them, so they never try to break free.'

The man was amazed. These animals could at any time break free from their bonds but because they believed they couldn't, they were stuck right where they were."

Chapter 15:

8 Habits That Help You Live Longer

Habits define who you are. Each habit influences your life on a positive and negative dimensions. After all, smoking a cigarette is a habit, and so are long hours of jogging. The behaviors that negative you from attaining your full potential also shorten your life.

Exercising, consuming nutritious meals, meditating, among others, makes our lives better in immeasurable ways. Our habits take over as an autopilot when our physical and mental abilities ebb and flow with age. This is especially true if you are old enough to understand the importance of habits but still young enough to make your positive habits count. As you get older, you'll find yourself relying more and more on your habits. Create good habits, and they will serve as the autopilot on which you will trust to stay healthy, active, and engaged.

As you create and stick to that habit you love, keep longevity and quality life your ultimate goal. Even if you've had bad habits in the past, now is the moment to break them.

Here are 8 habits that could help you live a longer life.

1. Exercise Regularly

Studies show that frequent, intense exercising is essential for age and physical health preservation. Getting out of your comfort zone to engage in a challenging exercise will reap benefits in the long haul. Hopping on a treadmill at a snail-like pace will do you no good. Therefore, it would help if you stalled rigorous aerobic exercises, stretching to your habit menu.

The less flexible you are, the more likely you will trip, break your hip, and end up in a nursing home like Aunt Karen. Vigorous exercise and stretching your body are the best ways to protect yourself from preventable injuries and the physical ailments of aging.

2. Mind Training

Mind training is equally vital as body exercises as you become older. As you train your body, your mind also needs activity to stay in good form. Learn and challenge yourself to remain alert and possibly avoid dementia. There are many minds training exercises such as puzzles, or even Sudoku, or any mind-challenging tasks.

According to a recent study conducted by John Hopkins Medicine, staying in school longer reduces the prevalence of dementia in the United States, particularly among individuals aged 65 and older.

3. Keep a Healthy Weight

Maintaining a healthy body means that you are cautious of what you consume. Consider the foods that enhance your physical, mental and spiritual wellbeing by avoiding calories and refined food staff. A new article in Medical News Today by Catharine Paddock, Ph.D., advocates keeping your body mass index (BMI) under 25% if possible. Keep your body weight as healthy as possible! It will impact your longevity.

4. Develop a Positive Mental Attitude

Whatever your viewpoint is on your present living conditions, impact your life in the long haul. That is, your take on your current life significantly reacts with the functioning of your body and soul. Therefore, people who adopt and adjust to a positive stereotype about aging are likely to recover faster from any disability. As a result, according to a recent study published in the Journal of the American Medical Association, longevity is achieved by maintaining positive thoughts towards your current state of affairs.

5. Elevate Your Mood

As we become older, depression and anxiety might become more prevalent. Do anything you can to boost your mood, whether it's through exercise or exciting mental activity. Go for walks in the park, re-enter the dating scene, or volunteer for a cause you care about – in short, do anything that makes you feel better about yourself and the world.

6. Maintain Your Social Contacts

Maintaining a social connection becomes meaningful as you grow older. You don't need a considerable social network; an influential network is enough. Your family, accordingly, may be enough, but only if the members are happy and flourishing. The Inverse is very true! If you find that your social network is exceptionally negative, look for ways to create a new one.

Make friends of different ages who may have other interests than you and keep fostering friendships you already have or may have had in the past. Remember, that person you allow in your inner circle is equally important.

7. Take Charge of Your Life

Rather than being a spectator, own your life. Don't just sit and watch the world pass you. Just get out and about, engage in activities that matter at every stage of your life. This means doing what a 25 or 40-year-old does to avoid mid-life crises. It can be not easy, especially in today's internet era, where we can check what other people are up to at the hour without even leaving the couch. On the other hand, sitting on the sidelines will not help you maintain excellent physical or mental health. Make sure you're not only listening to other people's experiences; get out there and make your own.

8. Do Something Valuable

Having a purpose in life and living up to it is vital. The drive doesn't have to be extravagant or mid-blowing to be meaningful as most of us think. Some people find their purpose in being an outstanding grandparent, volunteering for a cause important to them, or even mastering woodworking or gardening skills. It doesn't matter what your goal is as long as you have one.

On the other hand, not having a purpose might lead to poor habits that negatively impact your longevity and mood. Consider this: if you don't have anything to do, you can end up sitting in front of the TV all day, or worse, falling into the meaningless emptiness of social media.

Conclusion

The great news is that you don't have to take multi-vitamins or pharmaceuticals-promoted drugs to halt aging, hunger yourself, and thirst to reduce weight, or buy the latest products promising increased brain performance. According to several studies, adopting basic steps in the short term can result in longevity benefits.

Chapter 16:

20 Positive Affirmations For Men

A positive affirmation is a statement about yourself that is phrased in the positive, present tense. It reflects an area of your life, emotions, or belief system that you want to improve or change. The potential benefits of affirmations are vast. Positive affirmations empower you to become the best version of yourself. They inspire you to act in ways that help you fulfill your potential. You can use positive affirmations to reprogram negative thoughts into positive beliefs. The ability to reprogram your beliefs about yourself has the potential to transform your life completely.

For an affirmation to be effective, it needs to meet four criteria. Each positive affirmation you use should be:

1. **Worded in the present tense**
2. **Positive**
3. **Specific**
4. **Personal**

You can create your own positive affirmations using this four-step framework. The benefits of affirmations are dramatically increased when you have created it yourself from an existing negative belief. Let's say you had a belief that you are unsuccessful in your job. Where focus goes, energy flows. If you keep feeding this belief, it will manifest as truth.

When you understand this, you can see how our thoughts really do shape our reality. Instead, you can use this belief as an opportunity to grow. Take that statement and switch it to its positive opposite. Rather than thinking: 'I am terrible at my job, I'll never get a promotion, my boss hates me,' you now think 'I am great at my job, I love what I do, and I always put 100% effort into every task

Whether you choose to formulate your own positive affirmations or use the ones I have created for you below, you must cultivate a daily practice. The best times to practice are first thing in the morning and last thing at night (or whenever you feel that you need to repeat them to start feeling better). During these times, your mind is more open and will absorb the statements on a deeper level.

It is best if you say them out loud while looking in the mirror. Speaking them to yourself affirms that you trust in yourself, and you believe the statements to be true. If speaking to them out loud is not possible, you can say them in your mind. Writing them out a few times a week is also beneficial. Try getting a journal specifically for this purpose. Another technique that you might find useful is to pin the written affirmations to the mirror or refrigerator, where you will see them often.

When you are just beginning with this practice, it may be easy to forget, so set an alert on your phone or in your calendar to remind you. Here are 20 examples of positive affirmations relating to different areas of life.

Choose the ones that resonate most with you. Once you feel that you have integrated those particular statements, you can select or create new ones for other areas you want to improve.

Confidence and Self-Esteem

1: "I feel confident in every situation."

2: "I like who I am."

3: "I am a good person."

4: "I am great at helping people."

5: "I feel valued by my friends and family."

Inner Strength and Resilience

1: "I meet each new challenge with enthusiasm."

2: "I am strong and stable."

3: "I think I can, so I can."

4: "No matter what happens, I can handle it."

5: "I am powerful."

Positivity and Joy

1: "I radiate joy to everyone I meet."

2: "I see the best in people."

3: "In the present moment there are no issues, only peace."

4: "Happiness is a choice; today, I choose to be happy."

5: "I have the power to turn negative thoughts into positive beliefs."

Career and Success

1: "I deserve success."

2: "I can succeed at whatever I choose."

3: "I am good at my job, and I love what I do."

4: "I have great ideas."

5: "I am innovative and tenacious."

I hope that my guide to positive affirmations for men has provided you with a solid foundation for designing your perfect practice. Remember, to reap the benefits of affirmations, you should say them out loud every day and write them out a few times a week. Use any of my examples of positive affirmations, or for extra power, try creating your own using my framework. If you commit to a daily practice, you will soon notice the benefits in your career, relationships, emotional resilience, sense of self-worth, and confidence.

Chapter 17:

Avoid The Dreaded Burnout

Do you often lack the energy to get on with any new task and feel sluggish throughout most of your day? Do you feel the burden of work that keeps getting piled up each day?

I know we all try our best to manage everything on our hands and try to bring out the best in us. But while doing so, we engage in too many things and ultimately, they take their toll.

It is becoming easier and easier every day where people have more work than ever on their hands. And their sole motive throughout life becomes, to find more and better ways of earning a better living. To find more things to be good and successful at.

We all have things on our hands to complete but let me tell you one thing. You won't be able to continue much longer if you keep with this burnout and exhaustion.

Our body is an engine, and it needs a way of cooling down and tuning. So, what's the first step you need to reduce burnout? You need to get the right amount of sleep.

There is this myth that you sleep one-third of your life so you don't need an 8-hour sleep. You can easily do the same with four hours and use the other four for more work. Trust me, this is not a myth, it is a misconception about proven research. Your body organs deserve at least half the time of what they spend serving us.

We can refresh and better our focus and cognitive skills once we have a good night's sleep full of dreams.

Another thing that most of us avoid doing is to say No to anyone anytime. The thing is that we don't have any obligation to anyone unless we are bound by a contract of blood or law to do or say anything that anyone tells us to do. The more we feel obligated to anyone, the more we try to do to impress that person or entity with our efforts and conduct.

This attitude isn't healthy for any relation. Excess of anything has never brought any good to anyone. So don't give up everything on just one thing. Instead, try to devise a balance between things. Over-commitment is never a good idea.

The third and final thing I want you to do is to give up on certain things at certain times. You don't need to carry your phone or laptop with you all day. This only creates a distraction even when you don't need to be in that environment.

You don't need to train your subconscious to be always alert on your emails and notifications or any incoming calls all day long. But sometimes you just need to give up on these things and zone out of your repetitive daily life.

Doing your best doesn't always mean giving yourself all out. Sometimes the best productive thing you can do is to relax. And that, my friends, can help you climb every mountain without ever getting tired of trying t do the same trail.

Chapter 18:

Improving Your Sleeping Habits

Sleeping habits are an important part of growth. It is sad how most people have degraded sleep and it has turned out to be a measure of laziness. If you truly want to know the importance of sleep, deprive yourself of it for a few days and watch how your body will respond.

The importance of sleep cannot be over-emphasized. Have you noticed how fresh and strong you feel after waking up from a long and satisfying sleep? It is not the short naps and siestas during the day but the total rest that you get at night. You should constantly improve your sleeping habits. There are bad sleeping habits as well as good ones.

Here is a whole list about them and how they can be remedied:

1. Sleeping Late

Pushing daytime tasks into the night will not make you perform any better. Sometimes you may find yourself sleeping late because you did not realize time flies as you were storytelling. This is not enough justification. The remedy to sleeping late is developing a sleep schedule with consistent times to go to bed and wake up. Healthy sleep should be at least 8 hours long and uninterrupted. Depending on what time you want to wake up, observe bedtime time.

2. Sleeping With Tight Clothes

Some people sleep in tight clothes at night. This is unhealthy because sleep is a time of rest, and your body should feel free. Comfort during sleep is important. The remedy to sleeping in tight clothes is having nightclothes – a night dress or pajamas. They are highly recommended because they are tailored to factor in comfort during sleep. Do not sleep in jeans or clothes that you had during the day.

3. Constantly Checking Your Phone When You Go To Bed

Most 'modern' people are guilty of this crime – addiction to mobile phones. They carry their phones when going to bed (which is okay) but misuse them in bed. The misuse is that they start checking their social media and browser feeds when it is bedtime. The remedy to this misuse of mobile phones and other electronics is putting them aside when going to bed. This is not enough. Switch your phone to silent mode or turn on do not disturb (DND). Continued phone notifications will interrupt your sleep.

4. Listening To Music As You Sleep

The habit of listening to music on your earphones or speaker when you have gone to bed is unhealthy. Music may soothe you into sleep at the beginning, but it is a distraction that many people love. No matter how loveable it is, loud music will deprive you of sleep. The remedy to listening to music in bed is that you do not use your earphones and lower the volume when playing on the speaker. Soft music will make you fall asleep. You can also set the music to switch off after about one hour or so because you would have fallen asleep already.

5. Oversleeping

Sleeping is good but too much of it is unhealthy. Sleep must be regulated. You should neither go to bed late nor wake up late. Find a balance between the two and you shall optimize the importance of sleep. The remedy to oversleeping is setting an alarm. It will help you wake up early and as well as observe your sleeping schedule. Alarms are noisy and you should check-up with your roommate if they are comfortable with it (especially if it goes off early in the morning).

Conclusion

Sleep is important for your well-being. Great sleeping habits will make you sleep better and healthier. Observe the remedies to these five bad sleeping habits to be on the safe side.

Chapter 19:

Meditate to Rewire Your Brain for Happiness

Suppose you've ever read the book Bridge to Terabithia (or seen the movie). In that case, you are familiar with Terabithia – an imaginary world that the main characters, Jesse and Leslie, create as a haven. It is somewhere they can go to be free from the cares and worries of the world.

Meditation has given me a Terabithia. I have created a clearing of calm and tranquility that I can enter into within seconds whenever I feel the need. I have a refuge no matter where I am or what I am doing. The worries of the world no longer threaten me. Except this mental place isn't imaginary, and it isn't populated with trolls and wild creatures – it is as real as the world we live in.

Since starting my meditation habit, my brain has been rewired for happiness, peace, and success. Here are just a few of the benefits:

I rarely become angry.

I find happiness in unexpected places.

I form deeper relationships and build friendships more easily.

However, by far, the largest benefit is that a deep, serene calm and peace is slowly permeating into every area of my life. At first, meditating felt unusual – like I was stepping out of normal life and doing something that most people find strange. I soon realized, however, that this wasn't true – millions of people meditate, and many successful people attribute part of their success to meditation.

Oprah Winfrey, Hugh Jackman, Richard Branson, Paul McCartney, Angelina Jolie... Any of these names sound familiar? All of these are famous meditators.

This list alone is powerful, but maybe you need a little more convincing that meditation is something you should try.

Michael Jordan, Kobe Bryant, Misty-May Trainor, and Derek Jeter are just a few successful athletes who rely on meditation to get them in the zone.

Rupert Murdoch, Russell Simons, and Arianna Huffington all practice meditation.

Arnold Schwarzenegger and Eva Mendez are just a couple more celebrities that make meditation a daily habit.

Meditation Reduces Stress

Are you feeling the weight of the world on your shoulders? Meditation is incredibly effective at reducing stress and anxiety. One study found that mindfulness and zen-type meditations significantly reduce stress when practiced over a period of three months. Another study revealed that meditation reduces the density of brain tissue associated with anxiety and worrying. If you want your stress levels to plummet, meditation may be the answer.

Chapter 20:

Putting Exercise First

In this topic we're going to talk about why you should consider putting exercise first above all else in your daily routine and the benefits that it can bring to your health and all other aspects of your life.

Many of us don't usually prioritize work as the most essential part of our day. We have work, family, kids, money, and a whole host of problems to worry about that exercise usually comes in dead last on the list of things to do. What we fail to realize is that exercise is the one thing that we might need most to keep us fit and healthy to take on the challenges that life throws at us each and every day.

I'm sure you all know the benefits of exercise. Doing it regularly can bring lots of benefits to your metabolism, alertness, energy, BMI, muscle mass, and so on. But what does it really mean?

Have you ever wondered why you are always feeling tired all the time? Or why you feel like you haven't really woken up yet when you're already sitting in front of your desk at the office?

You see, it is the time of your exercise that matters a lot too. A lot of successful CEOs and entrepreneurs actually make exercise the first thing they do when they wake up from bed. The reason is simple, it gets the body moving which in turns starts the engine that drives you out of lethargy and into an active physical state. As you move on a treadmill or do yoga early in the morning, your heart starts pumping faster which drives more blood into other areas of your body to wake you up.

And this sets you up for success because you are no longer in a state of slumber and sluggishness. Exercising first thing in the morning also has the added benefit of checking it off your list early so that you do not wait for the lazy bug to tell you not to enter the gym.

Sure getting up earlier to exercise might also be a struggle in of itself, but you do not necessarily have to travel to a gym far away to get your daily exercise. Simply stepping out of the house for a quick run or finding an empty space in your house where you will not be disturbed and begin a yoga routine that you can find on YouTube will also suffice. As long as you get the body moving and in a state of flow, you would have already won the day.

Putting exercise first above all else in your day also gives you a sense of accomplishment that you have taken the action to improve your health consistently. Losing excess body fat will also increase your energy levels and help you get through the challenges of your work day with greater ease.

If you find that exercising first thing in the morning is just impossible to do for some reason, make it a point to schedule it sometime before midday, preferably during your lunch break. Leaving exercise to the night will only trigger more excuses from your brain not to go as your will power gets depleted more and more throughout the day. From experience, unless I have booked a class that i can't back out of in the evening, more often than not I will find many more excuses not to go than if I had scheduled exercise early in the day.

If there is a sport that you particularly like, I also urge you to schedule more games with friends or family throughout the week as you are more likely to show up for them seeing that you already favour the sport over other exercises. In my case I love tennis and would almost never miss a session that I have scheduled. Gym and yoga on the other hand, I am more inclined to give it a miss if given the opportunity.

So, for those of you who want to operate in a higher state of mind, body, and spirit, I challenge you to make exercise your number one priority and put it at the top of your list of things to do for the day. You will find your mind will be clearer and you will know exactly what you need to do for the day as you flow with the exercise. Feel free to play your favourite music playlist as you work out as well.

Chapter 21:

Seven Habits of Healthy People

Everybody wants good health for themselves. Healthy people are the envy of their peers who struggle with long-term illnesses and recurring infections. They work optimally and produce the best results. What is the secret to being healthy?

These are seven habits of healthy people:

1. Healthy feeding

Eating healthy does not mean eating a lot of food. It is what you eat that matters. There was a habit of people starving themselves during the day so that they can eat food at home. When this was discouraged, they shifted to another bad habit – eating junk food. There are many excuses for it. Some say it is cheaper while others say it is easy to make and sweet. However, much is left unsaid. Healthy people do not eat junk food. The damage done to the body outweighs its sweet taste

2. Scheduling of Meals

Healthy people abide by one principle – every time is not meals time. There is a particular time to eat. After that, you have to wait until the time for the next meal. This is a high-level discipline that most people lack. The only ones exempted from this are infants because they are too young to understand. It is unhealthy to eat in between meals. Snacks and drinks are unnecessary if it is not mealtime. When you continually break this rule, you will gain more weight that will compound your health issues.

3. Frequent Health Check-Ups

Whoever instilled in us that the only time to go to a hospital is when you are sick did a great injustice. It has taken a long time for us to appreciate the importance of health check-ups. These regular hospital visits even when you are healthy helps to detect a disease in its early stages. Cancer, for example, is treatable if diagnosed early. You will live a healthier life if you pay attention to any slight discomfort that you may have.

4. Guided and Objective Exercises

Unlike most people, healthy ones do not exercise for the sake of it. They know why they are exercising and are guided on how to do it correctly. Physical exercise is not something you want to start under peer pressure. It should be well thought of beforehand. With a clear target during exercises, healthy people can easily achieve their desired outcome. They become healthier because they benefit from the exercises.

5. Not Straining

Straining is highly discouraged. It is a way your body is communicating to you that something is not fine. There is no bravery in continually straining because you will hurt yourself more. It is healthy to change to a more comfortable position as you are doing your work.

6. Take Plenty of Water

Water is not a beverage. You are not supposed to take water because you feel like doing it. Taking plenty of water is necessary to keep you hydrated. It also helps to keep your kidneys healthy in their excretion function. No drink can replace water.

7. Having Enough Sleep

Sleep is not a luxury. Healthy people always have sufficient sleep. It is a way that your body rests and recovers from the previous day's activities. When you deprive your body of sleep, it will react to it. You will have a headache and general body fatigue. You risk falling sick if you continue missing enough sleep.

Conclusion.

It takes a lot to be healthy. It may seem difficult at the beginning, but it gets easier with time. Do not give up midway because you will not reap the benefits of your efforts.

Chapter 22:

Why Seeking Habits Can Motivate You Better

Our outcomes in life are often a lagging measure of our habits. We think that the things that need to change in our life are the numbers in our bank or the numbers on our scorecard. But the truth is that what needs to change is our habits.

Take this for a moment. If you have a messy life and a messy environment, you are prone to remain messy and act messy not only in your bedroom but everywhere you go and interact with the environment.

If you are used to piling up things in a corner and never trying to arrange or clean anything, it means you are not motivated enough to bring a change for the better. It means you are content with what you have, and you feel safe in your unorganized world.

If you feel this way, let this be your own diagnosis, that you are depressed and have no motive to do anything at any time. You always crawl back into your clumsy world because you have given up on the world being a better place for you.

I know it gets hard sometimes, but it doesn't mean you cannot soften things out.

What you are lagging in is not the goals that you wish or wished to pursue one day. Achieving a goal will make your life easier or happier for a short interval of time. But you don't want a piece of the cake, do you? We all want the whole cake for ourselves!

So how do we do that? It's easy!

Start chasing your passions and your habits. Go looking for new ones. Look for better habits in other people. Follow the people who seem free and independent. Those people have something going on for them that you are still looking for. Those deeds and practices will prove to be helpful for you too.

The process of doing things right is the right approach towards life. If your way of living your life is a positive set of traits, you are meant to live a fulfilling life. And you will get motivated to do more and better for not only you but also for the people surrounding you.

You don't need to lose weight if you train yourself to eat healthy in the first place. You don't need to earn more money, you need to control your spending habits. You don't need more money, you only need better financial baits and then you will always have enough money saved to manage any financial distress.

You don't need to try to do a thing like completing a marathon, writing a book, becoming a CEO. The goal is to become fit enough to compete for a marathon. The goal is to become a writer. The goal is to be eligible and talented enough that companies pursue your leadership.

Once you have adapted the behavioral and habitual identity, you are not really changing, rather you are acting in alignment with the type of person you already see yourself to be!

Chapter 23:

Why Considering Therapy Could Be An Option

Telling someone they should go to therapy or that they need therapy can be <u>stigmatizing</u>. It may be difficult to watch a loved one deal with mental health challenges, but it's important for people to choose to seek help on their own—as long as they aren't putting themselves or anyone else in danger.

Encouraging someone you care about to look into possible therapy options, even offering to review potential therapists with them, is generally a better way to show support. People who feel forced into therapy may feel resistant and find it harder to put in the work needed to make change.

While therapy can help people work through issues that lead to thoughts of <u>suicide</u>, it's usually not the best option for people in crisis. If you are in crisis, you can get help right away by reaching out to a suicide helpline through phone, text message, or online chat. You may be encouraged to call or visit the nearest emergency room. A therapist can help support you going forward, once you are no longer in crisis.

When any type of mental health or emotional concern affects daily life and function, therapy may be recommended. Therapy can help you learn about what you're feeling, why you might be feeling it, and how to cope.

Therapy also offers a safe place to talk through life challenges such as breakups, grief, parenting difficulties, or family struggles. For example, couples counselling can help you and your partner work through relationship troubles and learn new ways of relating to each other. Note that crisis resources, not couples counselling, are typically recommended for abusive relationships.

It may take some consideration before you decide you're ready for therapy. You might want to wait and see if time, lifestyle changes, or the support of friends and family improves whatever you're struggling with.

If you experience any of the following emotions or feelings to the extent that they interfere with life, therapy may help you reduce their effects. It's especially important to consider getting help if you feel controlled by symptoms or if they could cause harm to yourself or others.

1. **Overwhelm.** You might feel like you have too many things to do or too many issues to cope with. You might feel like you can't rest or even breathe. Stress and overwhelm can lead to serious physical health concerns.

2. **Fatigue.** This physical symptom often results from or accompanies mental health issues. It can indicate depression. Fatigue can cause you to sleep more than usual or have trouble getting out of bed in the morning.

3. **Disproportionate rage, anger, or resentment.** Everyone feels angry at times. Even passing rage isn't necessarily harmful. Seeking support to deal with these feelings may be a good idea when they don't pass, are extreme compared to the situation, or if they lead you to take <u>violent</u> or potentially harmful actions.

Chapter 24:

The Healing Power Of Nature

The Gift of Nature

The greatest gift the universe has put on our way is nature. Mother nature is there for us even when everything is against us. Nothing matches her benevolence. Her rich soil gives food to everyone who plants, her trees provide fresh air to breathe as well as attract rain from the clouds, and she is also home to the undomesticated animals.

Although we hardly appreciate nature enough, she has never ceased to look after us. Nature is also a source of medicine when we fall sick. Herbal medicine from indigenous trees is her gift to humanity. You can trust her to take care of you when things are difficult.

What Goes Around Comes Around

The principle of the universe is that what you do to people shall eventually come back to you. Whether good or bad, nature pays back in equal measure. Before you think of mistreating someone, be ready for payback time. It can only delay but is inevitable.

Consider people you meet as an investment. The more you invest, the higher the returns you get. The law of attraction defines how the universe operates. Good attracts good and evil attracts her mate.

Nature's Healing Process

Nature heals our pain and disappointments as a caring mother does. It is normal to feel let down or to lose something we treasure. Our family and friends can stand by us through such difficult times but there is only so much they can do.

They will console us but cannot take away our pain. Only nature can. It is constant throughout our struggles.

It heals us following these steps:

1. Grieving Stage

Unlike our family and friends who will want to replace our pain with happiness, nature allows us to grieve for our loss. Feeling lonely when we lose someone we love or the tender bid we wanted so badly is a normal part of life.

We want to withdraw from people because we feel that they cannot understand our pain. For a moment, their consolation seems fake (although it is not). Nature seems like the only one that relates to what we are going through.

2. Anger Stage

Anger comes after grief. Our loss makes us angry at everything and everyone for no reason. We fight people who want to help us. Sometimes we also blame them for our misfortunes. We find solace in our solitude. Our hearts go out to inanimate objects and nature's soothing calmness.

In our difficulties, the universe encourages us with memories of people who overcame similar experiences. Their testimony of victory comforts us that we shall also overcome what we are going through.

3. Denial Stage

After getting angry at ourselves for what we are passing through, we deny its existence. We fail to understand why we are chosen to 'suffer' in the manner we are. The denial stage could last longer because time does not stop to wait for us. Life seems unfair and there is nothing we can do about it.

Despite the harshness of reality, nature is tolerant of us. It does not punish us for our anger. It gifts us with time – the only ancient true healer. Time heals all wounds. We accept our loss regardless of intensity.

4. Acceptance Stage

This is the last stage of nature's healing process. After we are gifted with time, we lick our wounds and live to see another day. The magic healer makes us accept that life is moving on despite our loss. The clock shall continue ticking no matter how sorry we feel for ourselves.

We start to rebuild our lives after accepting this harsh reality. Nature is the only friend who has constantly been there for us in silence watching us metamorphose into better people.

In conclusion, the healing power of nature cannot be underestimated. Life throws jabs at us once every while, but nature is our surest path to recovery.

Chapter 25:

The Downside of Work-Life Balance

One way to think about work-life balance is with a concept known as The Four Burners Theory. Here's how it was first explained to me: Imagine that a stove represents your life with four burners on it. Each burner symbolizes one major quadrant of your life.

1. The first burner represents your family.
2. The second burner is your friends.
3. The third burner is your health.
4. The fourth burner is your work.

The Four Burners Theory says that "to be successful, you have to cut off one of your burners. And to be successful, you have to cut off two."

The View of the Four Burners

My initial reaction to The Four Burners Theory was to search for a way to bypass it. "Can I succeed and keep all four burners running?" I wondered.

Perhaps I could combine two burners. "What if I lumped family and friends into one category?"

Maybe I could combine health and work. "I hear sitting all day is unhealthy. What if I got a standing desk?" Now, I know what you are thinking. Believing that you will be healthy because you bought a standing desk is like believing you are a rebel because you ignored the fasten seatbelt sign on an airplane, but whatever.

Soon I realized I was inventing these workarounds because I didn't want to face the real issue: life is filled with tradeoffs. If you want to excel in your work and your marriage, then your friends and your health may have to suffer. If you want to be healthy and succeed as a parent, then you might be forced to dial back your career ambitions. Of course, you are free to divide your time equally among all four burners, but you have to accept that you will never reach your full potential in any given area.

Essentially, we are forced to choose. Would you rather live a life that is unbalanced but high performing in a certain area? Or would you rather live a life that is balanced but never maximizes your potential in a given quadrant?

Option 1: Outsource Burners

We outsource small aspects of our lives all the time. We buy fast food, so we don't have to cook. We go to the dry cleaners to save time on laundry. We visit the car repair shop, so we don't have to fix our automobile.

Outsourcing small portions of your life allow you to save time and spend it elsewhere. Can you apply the same idea to one quadrant of your life and free up time to focus on the other three burners?

Work is the best example. For many people, work is the hottest burner on the stove. It is where they spend the most time, and it is the last burner to get turned off. In theory, entrepreneurs and business owners can outsource the work burner. They do it by hiring employees.

The Four Burners Theory reveals a truth everyone must deal with: nobody likes being told they can't have it all, but everyone has constraints on their time and energy. Every choice has a cost.

Which burners have you cut off?

Chapter 26:

6 Signs Your Mental Health is Getting Worse

If you typically have <u>mild</u> or intermittent depression symptoms, you might notice immediately if they suddenly become more severe or persistent. Still, the different types of depression can involve a <u>range of symptoms</u>, and changes might creep up slowly instead of falling on you all at once. You might not always recognize small but steady changes in your day-to-day mood until you suddenly feel a whole lot worse than you usually do.

If any of the following signs sound familiar, it's worth talking to your primary care doctor, therapist, or another healthcare professional about a new approach to treatment. If you haven't yet started treatment for depression, talking to a therapist about these symptoms is a good next step.

1. Almost Nothing Sparks Your Interest

Depression commonly involves a decrease in your energy levels and a loss of pleasure in your favourite hobbies and other things you usually enjoy. As you work toward recovery, you'll usually find your interest in these activities slowly begins to return, along with your energy.

2. With Worsening Depression, You Might Notice the Opposite

It may not just seem difficult to find the motivation for <u>exercise</u>, socializing, and other hobbies. <u>Anhedonia</u>, or difficulty experiencing joy and pleasure, is a core symptom of depression.

You might also have trouble mustering up enough energy to go to work or take care of basic responsibilities, like paying bills or preparing meals. Even necessary self-care, like showering and brushing your teeth, might feel beyond your current abilities.

3. You Spend More Time Alone

With depression, you might find it challenging to enjoy the company of others for a number of reasons. You may not feel up to socializing simply because you have less energy. <u>Emotional numbness</u> can make the social interactions you usually enjoy seem pointless.

Feelings of <u>guilt</u>, irritability, or worthlessness can also complicate your mood and make avoidance seem like the safer option. There's nothing wrong with <u>spending time alone</u> when you enjoy it. An increasing sense of <u>loneliness</u>, on the other hand, can make your mood even worse. You might begin to feel as if no one understands or cares about your experience.

4. Your Mood Gets Worse at Certain Times Of Day

Changes in how you experience symptoms might also suggest worsening depression. Your symptoms may have previously remained mostly stable throughout the day. Now, you notice they intensify in the morning or evening. Or perhaps they feel much worse on some days instead of remaining fairly consistent from day to day.

5. You Notice Changes in Eating And Sleeping Patterns

Depression often affects appetite and sleep habits. When it comes to appetite changes, you might find yourself eating more than usual. You could also lose your appetite entirely and feel as if you have to force yourself to eat.

Sleep changes often happen on a similar spectrum. You could have a hard time staying awake and feel exhausted enough to sleep all day — but you could also struggle to fall asleep or wake up often throughout the night.

Trouble sleeping at night can mean you need to nap during the day to catch up, so you might end up drifting off at unusual times. This can affect your energy and concentration and further disrupt your sleep.

6. Intensifying Emotional Distress

If you have depression, you'll likely notice the following:

- hopelessness
- sadness
- a pessimistic outlook or catastrophic thinking
- feelings of guilt, shame, or worthlessness
- a sense of numbness
- problems with concentration or memory
- These feelings sometimes increase over time, so you might find yourself:
- fixating on negative thoughts
- worrying what others think of you or believing loved ones consider you a burden
- crying more often
- considering self-harm as a way to ease distress or numbness
- having frequent thoughts of suicide, even if you don't intend to act on them

If this distress persists or continues to get worse even with treatment, connect with a healthcare professional right away. It's not unusual for mental health symptoms to fluctuate over time. These changes may not always have a clear cause. Sometimes, though, they happen in response to specific triggers.

A few factors that could help explain worsening depression symptoms include:

- Stress
- Your treatment plan
- A different mental health condition
- Medication side effects
- Substance use

Chapter 27:

7 Signs You Are Emotionally And Mentally Exhausted

Riding the tumultuous rollercoaster known as life can be exhausting at times. You're high up one minute, and then you're back down where you started the next. When the lows outnumber the highs, though, the journey becomes boring. Instead, you'll be completely depleted on almost every level. Many people get intellectually and emotionally weary, resulting in many unpleasant symptoms. These symptoms may interfere with your daily routine, hurting productivity and relationships. If you see these indications, it's conceivable you're going through a difficult time in your life:

1. You Are Easily Irritated

You've been impacted by the tiniest of things recently. Negativity is everywhere around you, and it irritates you at any moment. You tend to lose your cool. As the days pass, you begin to lose hope. You become increasingly annoyed due to your ineptitude and lack of power. Unfortunately, this can lead to venting your frustrations on those closest to you, who don't necessarily deserve it.

2. You Always Feel Low and Lack Motivation In Your Life

You always get the feeling that something terrible will happen. You've lost hope in life, and nothing can persuade you to keep going. You believe you are unable to complete the task at hand. You're having trouble finding the motivation you require. Goals that once motivated you to work hard are no longer sufficient. This is especially tough to deal with at work or school when deadlines for various activities or assignments are looming. However, if you are not driven to complete those tasks, you will not complete them on time... and they will pile up, causing you to procrastinate even more. This could result in you failing classes or receiving work warnings. But if you're numb, you're not going to give a damn about that, are you?

3. You Experience Fits of Anxiety Quite Often

You are becoming increasingly stressed as a result of your exhaustion. Anxiety attacks are growing commonplace. You become overly concerned. You get anxious over the tiniest of things.

4. You Can't Sleep Properly

You frequently feel as if you are in the wrong place. The overwhelming sense of tiredness makes it difficult to quiet your mind and fall slumber. As a result, insomnia becomes another item on the to-do list. You are always exhausted, and all you want to do is sleep, yet you cannot do so. Why? Because your mind is racing, and you can't seem to break the cycle. Just as you begin to fall off, some anxiety will interrupt and jolt you awake, preventing you from getting that much-needed rest... compounding the exhaustion that is already draining you dry.

5. You Sense a Kind Of Detachment

You no longer feel a connection to anyone or anything. Nothing has an impact on you. You are neither happy nor sad. It's as if you're just a body with no feelings. You've become deafening. Whatever you're dealing with has sapped your energy to the point that you can't experience the emotions you normally do when confronted with a scenario or subject. This is similar to depression; however, instead of being burdened by emotion, you're burdened by the lack of it.

6. You Cry for No Reason At All

If you've reached the stage when having toothpaste come from your toothbrush first thing in the morning causes you to burst out shouting... That is not acceptable. We lose the ability to cope with hard situations when we are physically and psychologically weary, and routine day-to-day stress is amplified. It's acceptable if you've found yourself sobbing in front of coworkers, friends, or even strangers.

7. You Feel Dizzy and Nauseous

Nausea and dizziness are indicators that you need to rest and getting enough of it should be your top concern. These things occur due to your body's inability to cope with the stress and resulting in a breakdown. When a person has a mental breakdown, it is natural for them to become physically ill. This is especially true if you carry worry in your stomach or tighten your muscles instinctively to protect yourself from whatever is bothering you.

Conclusion

You can assist lessen the symptoms of emotional tiredness by making some lifestyle modifications. These tactics will be difficult to use at first, but they will get easier as you develop healthy habits. Small changes in your daily routine can help you manage your symptoms and avoid emotional fatigue. Once you've identified the symptoms of emotional weariness, work on eliminating them from your life.

Chapter 28:

8 Ways For Stress Relief

From minor to major issues, stress is naturally part of life. Even when the current circumstances have highlighted the rising stress levels, the phenomenon is not new. And while you may have no control over your circumstances, you control how you react to them. Stress can gravely take a toll on your overall health if it becomes chronic or overwhelming. In fact, according to a study that was conducted in 2012, unmanaged daily stress increases the likelihood of developing chronic health problems 10 years down the road.

So, is stress becoming more infuriating and upsetting? Is it affecting your mental peace and overall healthy? Relieving your daily stress is the most pleasing way of restoring serenity and calmness. Simply put, resort to the following easy, and proven stress relief techniques.

Here are 8 ways for stress relief.

1. Log Off, Stay Unplugged

Relieving stress is possible by simply pressing the "turn off" button on your phone. In the same efforts you put to control your diet, do the same to your social media interactions especially in the first hour of your day. Take command of the first hour by clearing your mind, setting motives, stretching, and hydrating. Doing so allows you to gain clarity and control of the entire day.

2. Take Charge

One of the primary causes of stress is losing control over one's circumstances. Taking control is an empowering act in and of itself, and it's a necessary step toward finding a solution that calms you down. Every issue has a solution. And if you remain passive, blaming yourself for being in that situation, you are in for the worst.

3. Exercise

Although exercising cannot erase all your stressful thoughts
permanently, it will help you relieve the intensity and thus allowing you
to handle the problems more calmly. In a recent Medicine and Science
in sports and exercise journal, exercising is found to be the most
accurate and healthy way of dealing or relieving stress. The journal
suggests moderate physical exercises like running, dancing, and spinning
as stress relievers.

4. Resort to Healthy Drinking and Eating Lifestyle

To cope with stress, we frequently turn to excessive alcohol or
overeating. Yes, these habits are relaxing in the short term, but they
increase stress in the long haul. Furthermore, they will degrade your
health. Instead, resort to a healthy eating and drinking plan.

5. Try Something New

Establishing new goals or challenging yourself, such as learning a
foreign language, volunteering, or participating in a sport, can enable
you to build confidence. You also lower or relieve tension while
participating in such activities. Continued learning makes you a more

emotionally resilient person. It equips you with knowledge and motivates you to act rather than sit back and just do nothing.

6. Leave the Work-Life at Your Office

A person who can leave their professional life at the office to savor their personal life can effectively deal with daily stress. Strike a work-life balance and mindset whereby both are adding value to your life. Don't be a person whose career defines who you are.

7. Accept Change

Change is never easy to accept or incorporate into one's daily life. And changing a problematic situation that you've found yourself in isn't easy. However, to move forward positively and avoid becoming entangled in that situation, you must accept change. The goal is to avoid wasting time on things that drain your energy and make you unhappy because you need to be productive and add value to your life. Just prioritize things you are in control of and leave the rest to Mother Nature.

8. Laugh More Often

Having a moment where you feel a good sense of humor won't take your pain away, but it will make you feel better. Laughter alleviates stress and causes profound positive effects on the body. It stimulates and deactivates the stress response. So, you can embark to good Netflix comedies, or hang out with funny friends.

Conclusion

Life is full of inevitable ups and downs, and it's all normal to experience stress at all walks of your life. To maintain your sanity, you'll need to bring down stress to a manageable level. Apply the above stress relief strategies at every stage of your life.

Chapter 29:

How To Deal With Stress

Stress is an inevitable part of everyone's life, and it's no secret that stress wears on your emotions and wreaks havoc on your physical health. Men face unique challenges and have unique needs for stress management. The circumstances are that as a man, you are juggling many responsibilities that you barely have time to manage stress; such that when you find yourself in a stressful situation, you handle it in an unhealthy way like overeating, drinking alcohol, or just laying around.

While it's almost impossible to do away with all the stress in your life, you can manage the situation and improve your health. A personalized care plan that includes time to recover and self-care can help you handle stress and motivate you to make healthier lifestyle choices. So how can you manage stress in your life?

Here is how to deal with stress.

1. Classify the Problem

First, classify the stressors in stressful situations rationally and how you responded to them. Keep a record of the events that caused your stress, including who was involved, the physical setting, and how you reacted. Taking notes can help you identify patterns in your stressors and reactions to them, allowing you to develop a stress management strategy.

2. Make Use of Mantras

Think of a mantra, and in this particular case, there are two effective ones; "I'm sure I can do it" or "That's not going to work for me." The former sentiment reminds you that you're capable of completing the task at hand. While the latter assures you that you are not always required to. Give your all to the things worth your time and effort, and let the rest go. You don't always have a choice, but when you do, it's okay to say no if saying yes will push you beyond your healthy limits.

3. Choose Your Battles

You don't always control external stressors, but you can practice restraint when it comes to internal stressors; that is the expectations you place on yourself. There's no reason trying to be all things to everyone and then feeling like a failure if you don't get to do everything.

4. Get Enough Sleep

A good night's sleep gives you a competitive advantage. Sleep is a form of self-care and one of the most effective ways to meet your physical, mental, and emotional needs. Giving up sleep is the same as giving up fuel. You get refueled after a good night's sleep, which helps you manage and reduce stress.

5. Figure a Way To Grow in the Challenge

Stress can cause you to think in a limited, pessimistic manner. However, this does not have to be the case all the time. Find your happy medium and calm those overwhelming or stressful thoughts. You'll probably become tolerant of stressors once you find a different approaching perspective.

6. Engage in a Physical Exercise

Exercising for your mental health doesn't have to be as rigorous as training for physical fitness. Almost any kind of regular exercise will get you there. Whatever type of exercise you choose, rest assured that it will lower stress hormones produced by your body while enhancing your mood-endorphins.

7. Chill Out a Bit

Unless you're in a life-or-death situation, a twenty-minute break won't hurt. Instead, take some time off and engage in things you enjoy doing. You can read, have a latte with a friend, or even enjoy your favorite show. Taking your mind off your problems reset your mind such that you return to them with a fresh perspective.

8. Get Organized

Nothing beats stress than being prepared and organized. It gives you a sense of control you may never imagine. Nothing exacerbates your stress like that piled-up paperwork, or a cluttered kitchen, or a backlog of emails. Set some time aside to address the issue or seek assistance.

9. Talk to Someone

Sometimes your problems become bigger when you keep everything to yourself. Get out, and talk to someone, be it a friend, or more so seeking professional help. Talking things out enables you to find solutions to your problems, thus triggering stress management.

Conclusion

Societal expectations are that a woman must multitask and do everything expected of a "typical woman" in order to earn a place or be valued. Resist and do things on your own terms because once you conform to such expectations, you're opening an avenue for mental health issues. Don't let this strenuous and frazzled world get the best of you.

Chapter 30:

8 Bad Habits That Make You Age Faster

According to a statistic given in an article in Globe Newswire, it's projected that by the year 2019, the global anti-aging market will be worth 191.7 billion dollars! Clearly, a lot of people are investing in products and procedures to help keep themselves looking young and beautiful. But, as with any disease or condition, prevention is always far better than the cure, and the same holds true for anti-aging. Unfortunately, there is no magic fountain of youth that will keep you young forever. But there are some particular habits and mistakes that, when avoided, can make you less likely to need anti-aging products and procedures. If you're a person who is concerned about an aging appearance, it's going to be important to avoid the things that make you age faster!

1. Processed Foods

Foods that have been highly processed and refined not only lack the nutrients needed by the body to support proper functioning, they typically also contain synthetic chemicals and other harmful ingredients that are detrimental to health. These processed foods cause faster tissue breakdown and other cellular damage that leads to faster aging. Additionally, when the nutrients that the bodily tissues need to function optimally are not optimally supplied, both the function and appearance of the skin and other organs can suffer.

2. Smoking

Smoking is a habit that not only wreaks havoc on your health but certainly speeds up the aging process. Even smoking one cigarette causes a huge amount of oxidative stress. This oxidative stress causes wear and tear on the body's cells, causing many issues such as aging, wrinkles, and other forms of degeneration.

3. Drug Abuse

Too much drug use of any kind causes internal stress on the body that again causes dysfunction, breakdown, and lack of optimal functioning. Depending on the drug, some can cause water loss, loss of healthy fat tissue, toxicity and more that can leave you looking older and frailer.

4.   Lack Of Hydration

Being improperly hydrated, especially chronically, surprisingly can make you look more aged. Water is essential for so many roles in the body that without enough of it, the function of the body suffers, which both directly and indirectly, can lead to quicker aging. Water gives your skin the soft, plump, vibrant, moist look that indicates health and youthfulness. Additionally, it helps internally to flush out toxins that can cause acne, red eyes, bags under the eyes, puffiness, and other ailments that certainly don't scream youthfulness!

5.   Not Getting Enough Sleep

Getting insufficient sleep is a major way to age yourself quite quickly! A chronic lack of sleep causes the body to shut down. Your eyes become bloodshot and red, baggy eyes, wrinkled skin, low energy, and many other symptoms that make anyone look older than they are! Sleep is so important both for health and for beauty that there's even the common saying, "I need my beauty sleep!"

6. Stress

Being chronically stressed is another habit that wreaks havoc internally. Stress typically is also associated with other habits that hasten the aging process. When stressed, people tend to sleep more poorly, eat more poorly, take more medications and drugs, and other such things that disrupt health and advance aging. Chronic stress keeps stress hormones elevated in the bloodstream constantly, which can have negative effects on the complexion of your skin, both the coloration and wrinkles, and causes red eyes, and an overall slumped, broken down and aged function and appearance. Having these stress hormones elevated chronically can lead to a number of health problems, the least of which is wrinkles and aging!

7. Being Physically Inactive

Being inactive is a sure way of making your body look and feel older than it really is. Sedentary living typically causes you to have poor posture, become overweight, lethargic, and just plain droopy! Keeping your body moving and strong does a surprising amount for keeping you looking and feeling youthful from the inside out. Individuals who stay active as they get older typically age much better.

8. Prolonged Exposure to UV Rays

Getting too much exposure to UV rays, either from being out in the sun unprotected too much or from tanning bed use, really causes a lot of damage to the skin, leading to wrinkles, sunspots and other damage that makes you look old.

By consistently maintaining a wholesome, natural, active lifestyle, you'll automatically be on a better track for avoiding fast aging. Following a diet of fresh, natural foods, being active, managing stress, and getting proper sleep can do leaps and bounds for helping you stay youthful!

www.ingramcontent.com/pod-product-compliance
Lightning Source LLC
Chambersburg PA
CBHW051024030426
42336CB00015B/2711